Finding Me
The Journey of Self Love

RIMA BHANDARI

HEARTFELT GRATITUDE

This book is more than just words on paper – it is a piece of my soul, a reflection of a journey filled with lessons, love, and transformation.

I am deeply grateful to the Divine, whose presence has always guided me. Every step of this journey, every realization, and every word written here has been a blessing I could only receive through this infinite grace.

To my husband & mother – my pillar of strength. Thank you for being there for me.

To my lovely daughter – you are my light, my inspiration, and the greatest gift of my life. Watching you grow has been my most beautiful lesson in love. You remind me every day of the magic within us and the importance of embracing life with joy, curiosity, and an open heart. This book is, in many ways, for you – to always remember that you are enough, just as you are.

And to you, dear reader – thank you for opening your heart to this story. May you find the courage to embrace your journey, knowing that you are always enough.

With love and warmth,
Rima Bhandari

CONTENTS

INTRODUCTION:
A LETTER TO THE READER

Dear Reader,

Have you ever felt like you're running on a treadmill, chasing success and approval, only to realise you're moving further away from yourself? This story is about Ananya – a woman who seemed to have it all, yet found herself feeling empty.

Through her journey, I hope to show you that self-love is not a luxury; it's the key to living a life that feels as good on the inside as it looks on the outside.

This is not just her story. It is ours.

With love and light,
Rima

CHAPTER 1:
THE PERFECT HUSTLE

Ananya's life was a finely tuned orchestra of chaos – every note, every movement, carefully choreographed to keep up with the relentless pace she had set for herself. At 31, she was the operations head of a leading technology firm in Bangalore's bustling Whitefield area. From the outside, she was the epitome of success – sharp, ambitious, and unstoppable. But beneath the surface, an exhaustion she refused to acknowledge began seeping into the cracks of her perfectly structured life.

Her mornings began at 6:30 AM with the shrill sound of her alarm. She'd roll out of bed, chug down a cup of black coffee, and dive straight into her emails – her laptop blinking with urgent messages from global teams operating in different time zones.

Her weekdays were a blur of morning traffic

jams, client calls, and endless meetings in sleek glass-walled conference rooms. Lunch was usually a quick sandwich eaten at her desk while multitasking. By the time she left the office, Bangalore's neon-lit streets were buzzing with nightlife, she was too exhausted to join.

Her weekends weren't any better. Saturdays were reserved for errands – grocery shopping at supermarkets, dry cleaning pickups, and trips to her bank. Sundays, though meant for rest, would often be spent prepping for Monday. Laundry, meal planning, and catching up on unfinished work consumed her time.

Ananya had everything society told her to aspire for – a high-paying job, an elegant apartment, and a closet full of designer clothes. Yet, at night, she lay awake feeling strangely disconnected, like a guest in her own life.

CHAPTER 2:
WHEN CRACKS BEGIN TO SHOW

One Friday afternoon, during a crucial client pitch, Ananya felt a wave of dizziness. Her hands shook as she clicked through slides, her throat dry. She forced herself to continue, clicking through the slides with a rehearsed confidence. But she could feel it – her body betraying her, exhaustion settling into her bones like a weight she could no longer ignore.

When the meeting finally ended, the room erupted into handshakes and murmurs of approval. Ananya barely heard them. Her head was spinning, her heart pounding too fast.

After the meeting, she rushed to the restroom and splashed water on her face. Staring at her reflection, she saw someone she barely recognised – Her usually bright eyes were dull, sunken beneath the weight of sleepless nights. Her skin looked pale, her jaw clenched with tension she hadn't even realised she was holding. Dark circles framed her tired eyes like bruises from a battle she had been fighting for far too long.

That evening, while catching a cab back home, she received a call from her mother.

"You work too much, Anu," her mother said. "When was the last time you visited us? We miss you."

"I'll come soon, Mom," Ananya replied, knowing it was a lie.

Her mother's words lingered. Ananya realised she couldn't remember the last time she'd laughed or done something for herself.

As the cab pulled up to her apartment, she sat there for a moment, gripping the phone in her lap, staring at her reflection in the glass.

The cracks were beginning to show.

And for the first time, she wasn't sure how much longer she could hold everything together.

CHAPTER 3:
THE MIRROR NEVER LIES

The following Sunday morning, Sun streamed through the curtains of Ananya's apartment, casting long golden rays across the wooden floor. The city outside buzzed with life, but inside, her home felt still, almost suffocating.

A strange heaviness had settled in her chest. A restlessness she couldn't quite name. And so, in an attempt to distract herself, she decided to declutter.

She started with her bedside drawer, pulling out old receipts, forgotten chargers, and scattered notes scribbled in moments of urgency. But as she reached deeper, her fingers brushed against something cold and smooth. She found a compact mirror. She recognised the mirror instantly. It was a gift from her mother, given to her years ago when she had first moved to Bangalore for work. She unfolded the note with trembling fingers.

"When you feel lost, look within."

She gazed into the mirror, expecting to see herself. Instead, memories surfaced – of her childhood in Mumbai. She remembered the long summer afternoons spent by the Juhu beach, dipping her feet into the cool water, reading novels under mango trees. She had always been a dreamer, a creator. A girl who found magic in the ordinary.

Tears welled up as she realised how far she'd drifted from that carefree, creative girl.

She had spent years chasing success, ticking off accomplishments like items on a never-ending checklist. Yet with each achievement, she had lost a part of herself. The dreams, the innocence, the simple joys – buried under deadlines and expectations.

Forgotten to nurture the person she once was. Forgotten to look within.

As she wiped her tears, a quiet resolve settled in her heart. She didn't know how, but she was going to find her way back.

CHAPTER 4:
THE COURAGE TO PAUSE

The following week, Ananya made an uncharacteristic decision – she applied for a week's leave. Her team was shocked, and her boss hesitated but eventually approved it.

The decision to take a break felt unnatural to Ananya. She had spent years moving at a relentless pace, convinced that slowing down was the same as falling behind. But after that exhausting Friday – the dizziness, the phone call from her mother, and the hollow feeling that refused to leave – she knew something had to change.

The first morning of Ananya's break felt unsettling. She woke up at her usual time, instinctively reaching for her phone, only to remember there were no emails, no meetings, no deadlines. The silence felt unnatural, almost heavy. She made coffee, but without the rush of work, it tasted different – too bitter, too still. She felt restless, as if she was wasting time. She had longed for a break, but now, without work anchoring her, she felt lost. By evening, exhaustion crept in – not from doing too much, but from doing nothing. She watched the city lights blink to life, realizing she had always been running, and stopping would take practice. Tomorrow, she will try again.

On the second day, she drove to a park early in the morning. Sitting under a massive Gulmohar tree, she opened a notebook she hadn't touched in years and began sketching.

The lines on the page weren't perfect, but they felt liberating. She spent hours there, watching joggers pass by, the sun filtering through the leaves, and the occasional chirping of birds.

CHAPTER 5:
CONFRONTING THE VOID

During her break, Ananya visited a counsellor, Dr. Aditi, on the recommendation of a colleague. Over the next few sessions, they began unpacking the layers of perfectionism that had governed Ananya's life. She traced it back to her childhood – how she had always been the "good girl", a straight-A student, the one who never disappointed. She realised her relentless ambition stemmed from a fear of "not being enough" & "being rejected".

She confronted painful memories of being a child who craved validation – from her strict father, from teachers who expected her to excel, and later, from a corporate culture that rewarded overwork.

One day Dr. Aditi asked Ananya,
"What would it look like to love yourself?"

The question caught her off guard. Love herself? The idea felt foreign, almost indulgent. She had spent so many years proving herself, measuring her worth by accomplishments, that she had never considered love – especially self-love – as something she needed.

"I… I don't know," she admitted. Dr. Aditi smiled gently.
"That's okay. Maybe that's where we start."

In another session, Dr. Aditi asked another simple yet powerful question. "Do you love yourself, Ananya?" Ananya's throat tightened.

No one had ever asked her that before. She had spent her whole life chasing love – from her parents, from teachers, from bosses, from society. But had she ever truly loved herself?

Tears pricked at her eyes as she realised she didn't have an answer. That night, as she lay in bed staring at the ceiling, the question echoed in her mind.

"Do I love myself?"

She thought about all the times she had been kind to others but harsh with herself. The times she had forgiven mistakes in others but held herself to impossible standards. The way she had abandoned her happiness for the sake of responsibilities, expectations, and approval.

For the first time, she saw the gaping void inside her – not one that could be filled with success or validation, but one that needed something deeper.

She didn't have all the answers yet. But for the first time in a long time, she was willing to ask the questions.

And maybe, just maybe, that was the beginning.

CHAPTER 6:
REWRITING THE RULES

Over the next few months, Ananya made small but significant changes. The transformation didn't happen overnight.. Instead, it was a series of small, deliberate choices – each one a step toward reclaiming herself.

She started saying "no" to unreasonable deadlines.

She slowly began setting boundaries – not just at work but in her personal life too. She no longer felt obligated to answer work emails at midnight.

She declined social invitations that drained her energy instead of bringing her joy. And most importantly, she gave herself the permission to rest without guilt.

She joined a weekend pottery class, and she also reached out to old friends – the ones she had once been inseparable from but had gradually drifted away from in the whirlwind of work and responsibilities.

She even started journaling – a practice that helped her untangle her thoughts.

Her colleagues noticed the change. She no longer seemed frazzled. Her creativity flourished, and her solutions became more innovative.

But the most profound shift happened when she decided to visit her parents. Her mother's face lit up as she pulled Ananya into a tight embrace. "You've lost weight," her mother said, concerned about lacing her voice. "Are you taking care of yourself?"

Ananya laughed softly. "I am now, Mom."

That evening, she and her mother sat by the Juhu beach, the golden sunset casting ripples of light on the water. For the first time in years, Ananya spoke openly – about the exhaustion, the pressure, the moments of feeling invisible even in her own life. When Ananya finished, her mother reached out, gently tucking a stray strand of hair behind her ear. "You don't have to carry the world on your shoulders," she said. "You were never meant to."

CHAPTER 7:
CHOOSING YOURSELF

Months had passed since Ananya had started making small yet powerful changes in her life. What had begun as an attempt to slow down had now become a way of living. She no longer felt like she was drowning in an endless cycle of work and responsibilities. Instead, she had learned to breathe – to pause, to feel, and most importantly, to listen to herself.

Her transformation wasn't instant. Some days, she still felt the urge to overwork, to prove herself, to be "enough." But now, she recognised those moments for what they were –

shadows of an old self that once believed love and worth had to be earned through exhaustion.

She had learned to say no – to impossible deadlines, to people who only reached out when they needed something, and most importantly, to the inner voice that once told her she had to be perfect to be loved. In its place, she had discovered a new voice – gentle, kind, and patient.

One evening, after finishing her work on time instead of staying late at the office, Ananya decided to take a walk. The streets of Bangalore, washed by an unexpected drizzle, shimmered under the streetlights. The air smelled of wet earth and freshly brewed chai from a roadside vendor. She wrapped her shawl around her shoulders and strolled aimlessly, feeling the cool droplets on her skin.

She passed by an old bookstore she used to love in her early career days but had long forgotten. On a whim, she stepped inside. The familiar scent of pages, ink, and nostalgia wrapped around her like an old friend. She ran her fingers along the spines of books, pausing when she found a worn-out copy of a poetry collection she had adored. She smiled, flipping through the pages, feeling a part of herself she had lost long ago coming back to life.

A short poem caught her eye:

"You are not what you do,
Not what they say,
Not the sum of others' expectations.
You are the love you give yourself
The whisper of 'You are enough'
When no one else is listening."

The words blurred as tears filled her eyes. She had spent so many years running, striving, and proving, forgetting that her worth had never been tied to what she accomplished. It had always been within her, waiting for her to see it.

Holding the book close to her chest, she walked out into the night. The rain had stopped, but the city still glowed – golden lights reflected in puddles, rickshaws buzzing past, laughter drifting from a nearby café. For the first time in years, she didn't feel like an outsider in her own life.

She felt present. She felt whole. And as she tilted her head back, letting the cool air kiss her face, she smiled.

She had finally chosen herself.

PRACTICAL TIPS FOR PRACTICING SELF-LOVE

1. Daily Check-Ins with Yourself

    Start each morning with a moment of reflection. Before diving into the day's demands, carve out five minutes to sit in silence and ask yourself:
    - How am I feeling today?
    - What do I need to feel supported?
    - Plan your day.

    Consider journaling your thoughts, which can help you uncover patterns in your emotions and recognize unmet needs. This simple act can empower you to be more intentional throughout your day.

2. Set Healthy Boundaries

Embrace the power of saying no. Identify the commitments that drain your energy, whether it's overworking, attending social events out of obligation, or maintaining toxic relationships. Prioritizing your well-being means learning to protect your energy and create space for what truly matters to you.

3. Rediscover Joyful Activities

Think back to hobbies or activities that once filled you with joy – perhaps painting, dancing, or hiking. Commit to engaging in these activities regularly, even if it's just for 15 minutes a week. Reconnecting with your passions can reignite a sense of purpose and happiness in your life.

4. Practice Gratitude

At the end of each day, take a moment to write down three things you're grateful for. This practice shifts your focus to the positives in your life, helping to cultivate a mindset of abundance and appreciation. Over time, you'll notice how this simple habit can transform your outlook.

5. Affirmations for Confidence

Challenge your inner critic by speaking kindly to yourself. Start each day with affirmations such as:
- I am enough, just as I am.
- I deserve love and happiness.
- I am worthy of rest and care.

Repeating these affirmations can help reinforce a positive self-image and boost your confidence.

6. Unplug and Reconnect

Designate one day a week to disconnect from social media and work emails. Use this time to reconnect with yourself, immerse yourself in nature, or spend quality time with loved ones. This digital detox can help you regain clarity and foster deeper connections.

7. Seek Help When Needed

Acknowledge that it's okay to ask for help. If you're feeling overwhelmed, don't hesitate to reach out to a counsellor or a trusted friend. Remember, seeking support is a sign of strength and a crucial aspect of self-love. You don't have to navigate your struggles alone.

SELF-LOVE: A JOURNALING SPACE FOR YOU

"You, yourself, as much as anybody in the entire universe, deserve your love and affection." – Buddha

Self-love is not just a concept – it's a practice, a daily commitment to choosing yourself.

But how often do we truly pause and ask ourselves, What do I need? How do I feel?

This journaling space is for YOU. A sacred moment to step away from the noise and listen to your heart. No judgment. No guilt. Just you, your thoughts, and your truth.

Take a deep breath, pick up your pen, and allow yourself to be honest.

Your journey of self-love starts here.

1. What does self-love mean to me right now?
(Is it setting boundaries? Is it giving myself rest? Is it choosing joy? Write what comes to your heart.)

____

____

____

____

____

____

____

____

____

____

2. If I truly loved myself, what is one thing I would stop doing?
(Would you stop self-doubt? People-pleasing? Negative self-talk? Recognise what holds you back and release it.)

____

____

____

____

____

____

____

____

____

____

3. When was the last time I felt truly at peace with myself?
(Describe that moment. What made you feel whole? How can you bring more of that into your daily life?)

____

____

____

____

____

____

____

____

____

WRITER'S NOTE:
A PERSONAL JOURNEY

Dear Reader,

This book is more than just a collection of words; it is a heartfelt reflection of my journey. There was a time when I felt trapped in a relentless cycle of exhaustion and self-doubt. From the outside, everything appeared fine – career success, meaningful relationships, and a life many would envy. Yet, beneath that polished exterior, I grappled with an unsettling emptiness.

Years ago, I hit my lowest point. Depression gripped my spirit, leaving me questioning my worth and place in the world. I was so focused on meeting the expectations of others that I lost sight of who I truly was. Every smile I wore felt forced, and every achievement I attained felt hollow, devoid of joy.

It wasn't until I stumbled upon the concept of self-love that my perspective began to shift. Initially, I grappled with the idea. How could I possibly put myself first when there were so many demands on my time? But as I embarked on this journey – setting boundaries, nurturing my passions, and quieting my inner critic – I realised that self-love is not a selfish act; it is the very foundation of a fulfilling life.

Self-love taught me to embrace my imperfections and find joy in the small, everyday moments. It empowered me to reconnect with my true self, allowing me to flourish in ways I never thought possible. This transformation was not an overnight miracle; it was a gradual, sometimes challenging, journey filled with discoveries. But every step was worth it.

This book is my way of sharing what I've learned, in the hope that it will inspire you to embark on your path toward self-love. Remember, you are not alone in this journey. You are worthy, just as you are. And you deserve a life that feels as good on the inside as it appears on the outside.

YOU ARE BEAUTIFUL AS YOU ARE!!

Love & Light,
Rima